INSIDE PEKING UNIVERSITY

Four Essays

Dr. Thorsten Pattberg

LoD Press, New York

"Language Imperialism is the translation of foreign key terminology into familiar vocabulary of one's own language tradition in order to claim deutungshoheit, to diminish another culture's originality, or to pretend to have full comprehension of a foreign topic by simply switching into one's own lingua."

"Calling Confucius a philosopher is like calling a whale a fish -wrong classification."

"The vocabularies of the world's languages add up, they don't overlap. Translation is something else."

"China is a living *shengren* culture."

                                        - Dr. Thorsten Pattberg

LANGUAGE IMPERIALISM
- IT'S SHENGREN, STUPID!

If you are an American or European citizen, chances are you've never heard about *shengren*, *minzhu* and *wenming*. If one day you promote them, you might even be accused of culture treason.

That's because these are Chinese concepts. They are often conveniently translated as "philosophers," "democracy" and "civilization." In fact, they are none of those. They are something else. Something the West lacks in turn.

But that is irritating for most Westerners, so in the past foreign concepts were quickly removed from the books and records and, if possible, from the history of the world, which is a world dominated by Western culture. As the philosopher Hegel once remarked, the East plays no part in the formation of the history of thought.

But let us step back a bit. Remember what school told us about the humanities? They are not the sciences! If the humanities were science, the vocabularies of the world's languages would add up, not overlap. Does that surprise you?

I estimate that there are over 35,000 Chinese words or phrases that cannot properly be translated into the English language. Words like *yin* and *yang*, *kung fu* and *fengshui*. Add to this another 35,000 Sanskrit terminology, mainly from India and Buddhism. Words like Buddha, bodhisattva and guru.

In a recent lecture at Peking University, the renowned linguist Gu Zhengkun explained that *wenming* describes a high level of ethics and gentleness of a people, while the English word "civilization" derives from a city people's mastery over materials and technology.

Tourists and imperialists do not come to be taught. They call things the way they call things at home. Then they realize that the names are not correct.

In many countries, adopting Chinese terminology is a taboo. Even the most noble-minded thinkers, such as the Nobel laureate Hermann Hesse, warned the Germans that "we must not become Chinese [...], otherwise we'd adhere to a fetish."

Next is "democracy," a concept of Greek origin. "Democracy" originally had little to do with letting the mob vote, lesser even so for the mob to rule the country; on the contrary, it meant that various, powerful interest groups should fight over the resources, each by mobilizing their influential supporters from the City.

While in China we still see a family-value based social order, in the West we find an interest group-based social order. In your family, you do not apply strict laws or make contracts; instead you induce a moral code. When among strangers who fight against other interest groups, you simply cannot trust them like your own family, so you need laws.

Up to the 20th century, the Europeans believed China was not a proper "civilization," because it had no police force, while China accused Europe of being without "wenming" because it lacked filial piety, tolerance, human gentleness and so on.

Finally, the *shengren* is one of the most important concepts in Chinese tradition. Since the Europeans never had anything like it, but refused to hold the candle to China; instead they omitted the *shengren* and talked about some lesser versions of Greek "philosophers" or Christian "holy men".

The English soon found a slightly better translation; they called the shengren "sages", from Latin *sapientia* –being wise.

The Germans however, the descendants of the Holy Roman Empire of German Nation, never had a concept for sages or sagehood. In their effort to christen China, the Germans called the *shengren* "Heilige" (saints), from Germanic *hailaz* –being holy.

Because of the many confusing translations, Confucius is said to be a paradox. He is not, he is a *shengren*.

As the ideal human being, the *shengren* is the highest member in the East-Asian family-based value tradition, a wise person that has the highest moral standards, called de, who applies the principles of *ren*, *li*, *yi*, *zhi* and *xin* (and 10 more), and connects between all the people as if they were, metaphorically speaking, his family.

Calling the *shengren* in Asia "philosophers", "saints", or any other familiar name is the greatest historical blunder since Christopher Columbus's discovery of "the Indians" in North America.

The modern Chinese word for philosopher, *zhexuejia*, is nowhere to be found in any of the Chinese classics. In fact, *zhexuejia* came to China via Japan, where it is pronounced *tetsugakusha*, after Nishi Amane first coined the word in 1874. Yet, the Western public is constantly told, through our highly subsidized China scholarship, that Confucius is a "philosopher" and that Confucian thought is "philosophy."

As Slavoj Zizek once said: "The true victory (the true 'negation of the negation') occurs when the enemy talks your language." The West would be irrational to adopt key Asian concepts. It would give away its *deutungshoheit* –the prerogative of the final interpretation. Think about concepts like "democracy" or "human rights".

In 1697, when the German culture was still young, the German philosopher Gottfried Leibniz famously argued that the Chinese were far more advanced in the humanities than "we are." He never specified, but I think it is all revealed when he urged all Germans that they must not use foreign words, but use their own language instead, in order to build and enlarge the German-speaking world.

And so they did. And so the Germans rose to the top. As expected, the Germans, the descendants of the Holy Roman Empire of German Nation, called Confucius a "Heiliger" (a saint or holy man). Now, that's convenient. But is it correct scholarship?

In the 21st century, is will be necessary to depart from some Western erroneous translations.

The East isn't just an appendix to the Western lingo; it has more to offer than the West could ever adequately translate. The key is to adopt foreign terminology. Only this way we can speak of a truly global language.

So that next time in international relations we could discuss how we're going to improve *minzhu* in Europe, and how to help America's transition into a descent *wenming.*

Maybe the West just lacks *shengren* after all.

DEAD IN TRANSLATION

Dear Friends, First off, I am truly sorry for your loss. The "Qingming Jie" looked and sounded too *Sinitic*; we had to replace it with the unambiguous, good-old "Tomb Sweeping Day". Sooner or later, all is caught in translation.

It wasn't meant to be. There are 1,3 billion Chinese stomping the earth, and also tens of billions of their ancestors romping the heavens. On *Qingming Jie*, those living and the dead come together for business. Yet, "Qing" and "ming" don't make it into Western press. Why?

Although I agree that translating *Qingming Jie* as "Tomb Sweeping Holiday" sounds all sweet and caring, some European missionaries went in for the overkill and cunningly translated *Qingming Jie* as their "All Souls Day", which then, of course, makes it perfectly resemble a Roman Catholic Holiday. We see we learn. Why not turn the table and planetize Chinese names instead? *Pinyin* with a vengeance, anyone?

As Confucius once said: If the names are not correct, language is not in accordance with the truth of things. It's known as the rectification of names, and it could well save *Qingming Jie*, if not an awful lot more.

Just as the German language is biblical, based on Martin Luther's German translation of the Bible, and Germany's descend from the Holy Roman Empire of German Nation, so is the Chinese language first Confucian and Daoist, and second Buddhist in spirit. Accordingly, German translations of Chinese key concepts are, and undoubtedly always will be, utterly misleading, if not outright diminishing East Asia's socio-cultural originality. Same is true in English.

The whole business of "Qing" and "ming", of course, is laden with unintended double entendres. When the tombs' pylons shine "clear" and "bright", that isn't just a Chinese metaphor for spring cleaning, but also the clearing of one's conscience. After all, what we do today is how we want to be seen and remembered in the future.

Yes, I do believe that the Chinese do not do enough to promote their own socio-cultural originality to the West. They, like the Japanese and Koreans perhaps, keep it all to themselves, so to speak, which is not always a good thing. I dread to think it is rather too passive.

The fact that I know *Qingming* Festival, or Dragon Boat Festival, or *Chunjie*, the Chinese New Year, is purely a function of my living here. In fact, had I not come to China, I would have never learned that China is a *wenming*; that is has *shengren* and *junzi*, that is aspires *datong*, and that Confucianism isn't a religion but is *rujiao*.

Although I must admit it isn't absolutely vital that "Qingming Jie", which has existed since the Zhou Dynasty in the 11th to 3rd centuries BC, survives and escapes Westernization. But some of you must be feeling watched by your ancestors shaking their heads, saying: "Tz, tz, tz, Lee, You've really let us down there."

China's ancestor worship is presumably a

direct corollary of its filial piety, *Xiao*. The Chinese show great respect for their parents and grandparents. Theoretically, this may be extended to the grandparents of their grandparents, then the next five hundred generations back to the sage who invented gunpowder, paper cut, and the back scratcher; and, ultimately, to the Yellow Emperor himself –Huangdi No. One.

Many Westerners cling to the superstition that the Chinese are superstitious. Some long noses may even believe that the Han still use oracle bones to communicate with their ancestors or ask them for signs of approval for marriage or immigration to the U.S.A. They also believe that the Chinese eat dogs and reuse tea bags. Ok, they do reuse tea bags. But the rest, bear with me, is grossly exaggerated.

It is certainly true that the sphere of family, *jia*, blends perfectily into everyday life and speech of the Chinese diaspora. Not even the One-child-policy of the 70th –meant to cut down population growth- could mute "family-language": The kids, though now solitary little emperors, still call all their friends "brother and sister" and all their parent's friends "Auntie and Uncle", and so on.

While the practice of ancestor veneration, *jing-zu*, *bai-zu* or *ji-zu* (depending on your geography), isn't universally just a Chinese reflex, yet all those masterful idiosyncrasies certainly are: its *fengshui* for burial sites, the quirks of *po* and *hun*, the obscurities of *yin* and *yang*, even the Buddhist finicky of 'ghost money', all make the Chinese *Qingming Jie* very unique and strike me as very un-European. And, according to my sources, 'Hell' in China isn't so bad at all.

Indeed, we in Europe bury our corpses in coffins and sink them into the earth, mostly located in our city's churches' backyards. We don't think of it as pollution. And while we do not offer wine and fruits, we are always ready to eat suchlike for picnic or barbeque at the gravesite. And, yes, we walk our dogs over cemeteries, and not for sight-seeing.

Loyalty for family isn't particular keen in the

West either. Chinese society is based on a family-value system, but Western societies are based on interest-groups. We prefer to lock away our helpless and unproductive elderly in nursery homes. As to the afterlife, the prospect of forever reuniting with one's ghastly family folks sounds awful and absolutely terrifying to the Western self-indulgent individualist.

Let us think carefully for a moment about *who* do we want to be remembered. Not what, but *who*. No matter what China is going to become, a semi-capitalist society, the world's next superpower, the inventor of great technologies, you will never be truly original if you always try to please or imitate the West.

Allow me to close with an anecdote. The scholar Albert Grünwedel spent his productive life translating the entire Sinitic tradition into the Germanic-biblical one, then went crazy and committed suicide. End of anecdote.

All translation is rather morbid.

LONG INTO THE WEST'S DRAGON BUSINESS

Had Siegfried or Beowulf not slain a European dragon but a Chinese *long*, those heroes would have committed an extraordinary crime. That's because the Chinese *long* is essentially a force of the good.

The *long* of China has a history (and etymology) of several thousand years and there are, according to linguist Michael Carr, more than 100 classical ones. Linguistically, it's a tragedy that many Chinese people, I mean the well-educated, English-speaking ones, are so readily prepared to call the long "dragons" - that's like voluntarily abandoning one's culture.

It is predicted that China will overtake the mighty United States in terms of the economy in a decade. Yet an ordinary Westerner has never heard about Lu Xun, doesn't know who Sun Wukong (the Monkey King) is, cannot tell a *shengren* from a *junzi*, has no inkling of *Xi You Ji* (The Journey to the West) or *Hong Lou Meng* (The Dream of Red

Mansion), or any idea about the correct name for that mysterious creature that's lavishly showcased throughout the international media these days: the Chinese *long*.

A *long* is a *long*, maybe even a *tianlong*, but please, please do not use "dragon". That kind of linguistic imperialism happened to your unique Sichuan *xiongmao* once, remember? Now it's a Western "panda".

It's not like asking every expatriate to recite all Chinese mythical creatures like *fenghuang*, *pixiu* and *qilin*. *Long* is good enough already. Say it loud: l o n g - as in longing, longevity, or long time no see.

For too long, the West has engaged in cultural pseudo-studies, making everyone believe that the Chinese language (all languages, really) just transports Western meanings uttered in some inconceivable foreign tongue. The reality is, if cultural studies were science, the vocabularies of this world would add up, not overlap. Translation is something else.

In a recent article, I explained how European missionaries and philosophers conveniently translated shengren as "philosophers" or "saints", and messed up cultural China. It's one of the greatest errors in the history of Western imperialism, only comparable, perhaps, to Christopher Columbus calling the Native Americans "Indians".

Because of misleading translations, there are now "philosophers" and "saints" all over Asia, yet evidently there isn't a single buddha, bodhisattva or shengren in Europe. Think - what is that probability? Whose version of history are we taught?

Western caricaturists love to depict China as the European-style dragon: huge and red (of course), clumsy and pear-bodied, fierce, with tiny wings and a small flame. That clueless beast virtually sits there on the cover of some magazine waiting to be slain by journalist Siegfried Weischenberg, the World Trade Organization or the Barack Obama administration.

The truth is, the Chinese long are majestic, divine creatures, snake-bodied (snake is often called a *xiaolong* (*xiao* means "little" or small") and embody happiness, wisdom and virtue. In the West, on the other hand, it's a virtue to slay the dragon for a happy ending. If the European "dragon" had been on the Yellow Emperor's mind, what sort of people the "children of long" would have turned out to be?

See it from a Western perspective: the French have the cock, the Germans the eagle, the Americans the bald eagle ... and the Chinese a blinking "celestial dragon"! Of course, every sharp Western pen is trying to pick on the beast, and hurt it.

Cultures have preferences: Most Western kids love dinosaurs, the "terrible reptiles", because they think they are cute (compared to, perhaps, mythical dragons). In China, "dinosaurs" are called *konglong*, the terrible version of a mythical dragon. Or, how about this one: a drakon in Greek is a serpent of the seas, while a *long* in China is a serpent of the skies or the seas.

Some commentators argue that the "dragons" are now becoming cute and sociable in the West, too. About this, I have doubts. I believe that for Western children the empowering aspect of the dragon's physique and (fire-)power is utilized as a tool against one's foes; they feel like beast-taming dragon-riders. Look at Hollywood and the game industry.

In short, the European dragons haven't become friendlier at all, they just have been subjugated. As long as Westerners call the Chinese *long* a "dragon", they will project their own cultural ideas on China.

Yet, if they used the correct word, *long*, it would remind them that they are facing something culturally new. And, finally, they would also be able to say the names of China's beloved kungfu stars correctly: Bruce Lee (Li Xiaolong) and Jackie Chan (Cheng Long).

You must protect your traditions. This is true for all people. English as a global language is fine but, ideally, only if it accommodates all concepts and all cultures ever produced.

Embrace the differences and varieties of cultures and value those concepts that matter the most. Protect them.

The *long* is precious.

INSIDE PEKING UNIVERSITY

A lot of people search endlessly for the secret key or a magic formula that would enable them to understand China. Naturally, at some point they will want to know how the Chinese are educated. The Middle kingdom has many prestigious schools, but let us take a closer look at Peking University, the mother lode of the Chinese *wenming*.

Wenming is often translated as "civilization", but that is misleading. In a recent lecture at Peking University, the renowned linguist Gu Zhengkun explained that "wenming" describes a high level of ethics and gentleness of a people, while the English word "civilization" derives from a city people's mastery over materials and technology. Think about architecture.

"Peking University", this term, is of course its Westernized name. So that foreigners can find its address. The Chinese themselves, however, call their institutions of higher learning the "daxue". Peking University is

Beijing daxue or *Beida*, Tsinghua University is *Qinghua Daxue* and so on. "Daxue is not a translation of Greek *universitas*," explains Professor Gu, but "a reference to one of the great Confucian classics, the *Daxue*". The *Daxue* is often loosely translated as "The Great Learning", but it is really this: an instruction manual on how to become a *junzi* and then, perhaps, a *shengren*.

The *junzi* is the ideal personality in China's family-value based tradition, while a *shengren* is its highest member, a sage that has perfected the highest moral standards, called *de*, who mastered the principles of *ren*, *li*, *yi*, *zhi* and *xin*, and who now connects between all the people as if they were, metaphorically speaking, his family. The historian Tu Weiming even calls the *shengren* "the highest form of an authentic human being".

The *junzi* and *shengren* of Confucianism are as clearly defined, unique, and non-European as for example the bodhisattvas and buddhas of Buddhism are. Yet the former are completely unknown to the educated

Western public due to erroneous, biblical and philosophical European translations dating back to the 17th to 19th centuries. As the historian Howard Zinn once remarked: "If something is omitted from history, you have no way of knowing it is omitted."

While a Western university's principle aim is to produce a skilled expert, a Chinese *daxue*'s principle aim is to cultivate an ideal character. Anglo-Saxon students often seem surprised when they hear that the Chinese daxue do not award PhD degrees or "Doctors of Philosophy". They award a "boshi", which literally means an erudite master.

The word for "philosopher" doesn't appear in the Chinese classics. Our so-called "Chinese Philosophy" departments in the West are reminiscences of the imperial age. In fact, the Chinese word for philosopher, *zhexuejia*, came to China via Japan not before 1874, where it is pronounced *tetsugakusha*.

As the great educator and linguistic sage Ji Xianlin once remarked: We practically know the West like the palm of our hand, but the

West's vision of the East is still a murky confusion".

Maybe, since the West obviously lacks the concepts of *shengren* and *junzi*, letting alone the *daxue*, we should adopt those Chinese concepts, out of necessity and by common sense, just as Japan and China back in the 19th century adopted the Western concepts like "artist", "scientist", and "philosopher". It's simple reciprocity.

Of course, some Western philosophers like Immanuel Kant and Georg Wilhelm Friedrich Hegel have traditionally played down Chinese socio-cultural originality. Western scholarship will always prefer European terminology to describe China because it wants to keep what the Germans call *deutungshoheit* –the prerogative of final explanation. Or, as Slovenian philosopher and critical theorist Slavoj Zizek once said: "The true victory (the true 'negation of the negation') occurs when the enemy talks your language."

Tourists and imperialists rarely come to be taught; they call things in China just the way they call things at home. Only, that is, to later put their feet in their mouths, because all is clear *mafan* and *maodun*, and nothing ever seems quite *meizuo* for them in *Zhongguo*.

Using the correct terminology often makes a huge difference, indeed: yes, a "Peking University", this architectural coloss, was founded in 1898, only recent by Western standard. Yet, the Chinese *daxue* can be traced back to its origins in the Spring and Autumn period, some 700 to 500 years before our Lord, Jesus Christ!

As Confucius once said: If names be not correct, language is not in accordance with the truth of things. It's known as the rectification of names. Educated in error, the people of Europe to this day have no idea what they are missing: The East invented tens of thousands of non-European concepts they may have never heard about.

China is a *wenming* with a Confucian love for learning. Peking University is a living *shengren* culture.

ABOUT THE AUTHOR

Dr. Thorsten Pattberg, a German cultural master and Confucian scholar, was born in Germany and studied Chinese, Sanskrit, Indian and Buddhism Studies at The University of Edinburgh, Fudan University, The University of Tokyo, and Harvard University. He graduated from the Institute of World Literature of Peking University, and is the author of *The East-West dichotomy* (2009) and *Shengren* (2011).

Inside Peking University is a collection of four critical and timeless essays on the Chinese concepts of *daxue*, *shengren*, *junzi*, *boshi*, *wenming*, the *Qingming* Festival, and *long* (the Chinese dragon). Dr. Pattberg argues for example that the *shengren* of East-Asia are largely overlooked: They are a class of their own, like the buddhas. To translate them as "philosophers" or "saints" seems imperialistic and all-too-convenient. The *shengren* are above philosophy and beyond religion –they are quite un-European, and so are the other Chinese concepts advocated in this book.

The cases presented in here are emblematic of the widespread abuses of translations in 'Cultural Studies' which, so argues Dr. Pattberg, have distorted the reality of cultural China and subsequently have helped the West to tilt 'World History' toward European sovereignty over definition and classification of thought.

The first essay, *Language Imperialism,* is one of the most widely read texts in East-Asia Studies today. It has been syndicated thus far throughout several media outlets such as *China Daily*, *Global Times*, *Global Research*, *China Today*, *Xinhua*, *Asia Times*, *Japan Times*, and the German Times (*Die Zeit*), among others.

Key concepts (in order of appearance):

shengren	圣人
minzhu	民主
wenming	文明
qingming jie	清明节
junzi	君子
rujiao	儒教
xiao	孝
jia	家
long	龙
daxue	大学
zhexuejia	哲学家

www.ingramcontent.com/pod-product-compliance
Lightning Source LLC
Chambersburg PA
CBHW071805020426
42331CB00008B/2407